SURVIVING SUCCESS

iX
indieXperts
PUBLISHING & AUTHOR SERVICES

SURVIVING SUCCESS

How ticking life's boxes will get you what you want
BUT NOT WHAT YOU NEED!

TIM WISE

First published 2024 by Tim Wise

Published by Tim Wise

Produced by Indie Experts
indieexperts.com.au

Copyright © Tim Wise 2024

The moral right of the author to be identified as the author of this work has been asserted.

All rights reserved. Except for the purposes of reviewing, no part of this publication may be reproduced or transmitted in any form or by any means, electronic or mechanical, including photocopying, recording or any information storage or retrieval system, without the written permission of the author. Infringers of copyright render themselves liable for prosecution.

Cover design and typesetting by
Ammie Christiansen, Fast Forward Design
Typeset in 11pt Adobe Caslon Pro

ISBN
Printed: 978-1-7635842-8-0
eBook: 978-1-7635842-9-7

Disclaimer:
Every effort has been made to ensure this book is as accurate and complete as possible, however they may be errors both typographical and in content. The author and the publisher shall not be held liable or responsible to any person or entity with respect to any loss or damage caused or alleged to have been caused directly or indirectly by the information contained in this book.

Some names and identifying details in this book have been changed to protect the privacy of individuals.

CONTENTS

How to Use this Book — 1

Introduction: The Radical Road — 3

1: The Social Requirements of Ticking the Right Boxes in Life — 13

2: Living Above and Below the Line - The New Paradigms — 19

3: The Concept of the Box — 29

4: What Do We Put in and TakeOut of our Boxes? — 39

5: Of Life, Love, and Learning — 47

6: Knowing Truth — 55

7: Story On, Story Off! — 59

8: Permission Givers — 63

9: The Line of Courage — 67

10: Beyond the Boxes — 71

11: The Final Word Life Lived in Amped Stillness — 79

Acknowledgements — 85

Wanting to know more? — 87

How to Use this Book

You will find that there are some things I talk about in this book that go deep and I've found there are simply not quite the right words to convey my meaning in places. So, I've made a few up and also played with the English language rules in places. For example, words like Un-tied are written to bring emphasis to being more than just separated - where one might use 'untied'. Un-tied by comparison is about (detaching). Stillness is written with a capital S – as are some other words – when I wish to convey that as being a specific state of being, not merely sitting quietly. So please forgive the playing with language if that means you feel I've misspelled some things, but these are in fact deliberate, as you will see by their consistency.

As you read my stories and gain deeper insight into the way I've learned to find a balance between Stillness and Amped states of being, I hope you find time to also sit and rest with these ideas and insights as they reveal themselves to you too.

It is not my desire to cause complication in your own thinking about these matters, but hopefully to help you see the simplicity of these and embrace them as and how they work for you.

Tim Wise

Introduction: The Radical Road

Are you a Searcher?

Do you wonder why you feel unfulfilled, thinking 'is this it'?

Is this all there is?

The alternatives may be that you are supremely happy, blissfully unaware, or just don't care and if this the case, this book is not for you. Put it down and have a nice day!

From a relatively young age I wondered how I could escape the suffering I felt on an almost constant basis. It's not that I had a harsh upbringing in any way. I was fortunate to have had loving parents who worked hard and only wanted the best for me and my two siblings… but this wasn't enough for me. I wanted more. And yet I did not know *what* was missing, I just knew that there was something to discover or find. I felt disconnected from my True Purpose and felt there was something missing. I believed there must be more but didn't know what.

My grandparents were both immigrants with successful small

businesses. They fled Nazi Germany and Russian repression respectively in the late 1930s.

From the time they arrived in Australia my father's parents were acutely aware of the perception of Germans in what was then a little town called Perth. It was about as remote as it was possible to be from the conflict that raged across the rest of the world as a result my father changed the family name from Weissenberg (White Mountain) to Wise to help protect the family. They were generous grandparents, constantly showering us with gifts, but also ensuring others they met would experience their giving nature too. I think having come from those circumstances, they were able to truly appreciate what Australia and Australians had to offer at many levels.

My father grew up to be a successful serial-entrepreneur who has raised money and started businesses of every imaginable type. He is a highly intelligent man who attained a PhD in Biochemistry and then threw off the lab coat and launched himself into business at the relatively late age of 30. He always demonstrated to me the diverse number of ways there are to make money and has instilled some good values that are what have shaped me and enabled me to thrive and grow through various challenges in my 50 plus years. My mother has often been described as a Saint, a stoic child of the 40's who has never ever complained and is always thinking of and doing things for others. She is loved and revered in equal measure wherever she goes.

There are two things in particular I have come to know that guide me. Until you lose something, you really don't know what its value was, and when your baseline is good – for example- food, water, living standards, opportunities, peace etc. - it seems natural from a mind-based state to just keep looking for more.

I am incredibly proud to be Australian and all that entails but I am also acutely aware that as a nation we must step up and share messages that will empower our people in ways that may not have been previously explored by the mainstream. Australia is so rich and abundant in resources and beauty, and maybe because of this we keep looking to the outside for our happiness. Once we have some boxes ticked that we believe reflect what it means to succeed, what is there to sustain and grow happiness without getting jaded or bogged down in disappointment by continuing to do the same old, same old? This book will tackle these questions head-on and explore what lies beyond this physical reality and how we can use it to become happier and more fulfilled.

One exceptionally hot day, even by Perth standards, I was leaving university after my last lecture for the day. I opened the door to my white 1975 BMW320 and sat back on the sizzling vinyl driver's seat when I felt the searing pain of a large acne cyst burst in the middle of my back - sorry for the graphic description if you're squeamish! This memory was extremely painful, both physically and psychologically, so much so that I can still recall the moment and the emotions associated with it like it was yesterday. My acne had been severe for about 3 years by then and served to always make me feel less confident around others. As a surfer and beach person I was always reticent to take my shirt off either at the beach or around a pool. it caused me so much pain, but in many ways, it made me who I am. We've all heard the saying what doesn't kill you makes you stronger. Acne made me realise that there has to be more to life than the physical because if there wasn't, I was going to have a miserable time and in many ways life was meaningless. I struggled to make sense of the idea that my life might be so shallow that it was acne which defined me.

***

Bob Randell, who is no longer with us, was an elder from Uluru, who explained that Kanyini is the connection that Australia's first nations people had with the country we call Australia. In his documentary by the same name, he talks about how white man systematically took away their connection (Kanyini) by taking them away from the region in which they grew up, taking them away from their family, taking away their culture and their land. He described in this beautifully filmed documentary, that his culture - like many wise cultures - says we are all connected and all one. As Westerners living in boxes, watching boxes and eating from boxes we have become disconnected from nature, our Kanyini, our connection to Self. This has become the new normal, but it is anything but normal! I believe most of us do not reflect on this enough.

Imagine going from a genuine connection to nature (a connection so deep that it not possible to distinguish yourself from it) and then being in a completely foreign environment and cut off from everything that was real and meaningful to you and who you identified yourself to be. The reality is that we don't need prison cells to be in prison, in fact we all unconsciously put walls and limitations around us and others all the time.[1]

Satsang - Learning at the Foot of the Master

Since about the age 16 I have been what could only be described as a seeker. I was attracted to many personal development courses, which led me into spirituality. I prefer to call it 'personal diminishment', because I feel it better describes how we really grow.

I remember in the 1990s being on a course called Future Warrior in which the facilitator mentioned the word 'Satsang'. It was a word that sparked intrigue, but also seemed familiar to me. That same week I was flicking through a spiritual magazine called Nova which was prominent in Western Australia at the time, when I stumbled across an advertisement that said ShantiMayi would be doing Satsang at the Shenton Park Council in a few weeks' time. I immediately rang a man named OM who was organizing the event and I made arrangements to attend.

Satsang is a gathering where you listen to a spiritual master and

---

[1] I highly recommend watching the 2006 Kanyani Documentary which is free on the internet.

ask questions relating to your life. These will often be centered on challenges that you're facing, with the ultimate objective of Self-realisaton and Enlightenment. It is important to get the proper guidance from the "real deal", someone who is already Self-realised and can act as a guide on one's own path. There are many pitfalls and misnomers on the path to realising your True Nature.

I was only in my early thirties and was the youngest at the Satsang gathering by some margin. It is amazing how our minds will make us think we are getting somewhere when we are really just going round and round in circles. It takes a Master to constantly bring us back to Self and remind us to keep going and growing.

I soon committed to be a devotee of ShantiMayi and later learned that I was in fact devoting myself to my own Truth and Awareness. I was realising who I was beyond the suffering and repetitive stories, beliefs and frustrations.

To start with however, I was more confused than ever as my body, mind and emotions started to realign to something I didn't yet understand.

I first travelled to India not long after meeting, ShantiMayi at that encounter in Perth. I remember arriving at Indira Gandhi International Airport in Delhi and being overwhelmed by the smells, the sites and organised chaos.

As I made the trip from Delhi to Lakshman Jhula at the foot of the Himalayas, I started experiencing sensory overload. My eyes were out on stalks as I took in the many sites, including people lying on the side of the road after being knocked off their motor bike, hordes of beggars who would come up by the side of the car pleading for money and food every time we stopped - which was often in the bustling traffic - bullocks towing carts carrying Indian men and woman, some who were talking on their mobile phones.

What a place! It felt surreal and magical - something inside me recognized there was something special going on. Over the course of the next few weeks, I attended Satsang at the foot of my master every day - the Master talked, and I the student listened to matters of the Heart and Truth. These were profound, and sometimes confronting teachings.

During the time I was in Lakshman Jhula there was something stirring in me, but I couldn't have told you what it was at the time. My teacher Amitabha and Master ShantiMayi, knew from their experience that whatever was happening to me was good, but it didn't feel that way to me. I was breaking!

I Can Only Describe it this Way:

I became very emotional from the high vibration I was immersed in. My nervous system was being affected by the high energy and it was purifying me, addressing the parts of me that were out of alignment with Truth. Everything became less certain, less concrete and old thinking, beliefs and stories within me felt like they were dissolving. At the time it scared me because I could not explain what was happening with my rational mind and it didn't feel great. I was rediscovering my connection - my Kanyani - but it was so unfamiliar to my regular way of living that my body was having a hard time dealing with it.

Since that first trip to India, I have been back a number of times and have always found it both confronting and beautiful.

The interesting thing about the Spiritual Journey is that is very counter intuitive, relative to our material world which is governed by stories, beliefs and formulas. There is no figuring it out with the same mind we use for seemingly everything else.

From those very first days of sitting at my Master's feet I have continued to go around in circles, only to keep coming back to the same fundamental Truth that what is, IS. That sounds simple because it is, but the mind does not want us to get there because that would mean that all the stories it generates to help us find meaning in things would no longer carry any weight, or at the very best they would be relative truths.

Experiences are important for what they teach us However experience in and of itself is only useful for the insight that it gives us into the Truth. We remember, we forget, and we remember again. It's constantly three steps forward and two steps back and eventually our dominant operating system becomes Truth, Oneness, Love as an experience, not a series of thoughts or beliefs.

My journey to find something other than my perceived reality at the time, has at times taken me down many rabbit holes as I explored the many avenues available to pursue an ultimate state of health, wealth and wisdom. This has brought me extraordinary pleasure and at times high levels of suffering which became my primary motivator. But it also helped me to develop the grit to carry on chasing an invisible Wisdom that to many (including myself) does not/did not always make sense.

This book is written as a guide for anyone who feels as though they are not living their True Purpose and feels that something unexpressed or unrealised exists in them. This is a book which shares stories of radical departure from the way most people see or approach the world.

Let's start with this:

- Who are you?
- Where are you going?
- How are you going to get there?

These are the three fundamental questions asked of me by one of my mentors some 30 years ago and to some extent I am still working this out. Or at least it seems my priorities change on a regular basis. I have never been the type of guy to stay in one lane if I thought there was a better or quicker way to get to my destination.

What is my destination you might ask? Well, that depends; sometimes it's health, sometimes it's family, sometimes it's money. Oftentimes it's self-exploration. With that said, one of the themes I have seen come through in my life, time and time again, is that I have always been trying to get somewhere, striving for success. And it is this striving that has shown me, repeatedly, that there is nowhere to get except right here, right now.

I have discovered that we work across several worlds with very different ground rules. In the West we tend to give the physical world our full attention. If you can't touch, feel and see it, maybe it just does not exist. However, we have no problems picking up a mobile phone or remote-control device and not giving a second to thought to how this can invisibly facilitate a call on the other side of the planet or change the channel on the television.

The physical world is where things appear to happen; you build a business, go to a job, buy that car or house, marry that guy or girl. You can touch it, see it, and feel it and therefore it must be the highest truth and there is a formula to creating all these things, right? Formulas such as setting goals, working hard, persisting etc.

However, is there a higher Truth which can help us in our lives to heal, feel and be happy as well as support our success in the world? Great Sages, Saints and Spiritual Masters tell us Self Realisation and Mastery of our inner world exists but what does this mean to the householder trying to work two jobs and or feed themselves and their family, take a yearly vacation and look after their ageing parents? As it turns out: a lot. And further to that, the time to tap into our invisible brilliance is now.

The extreme speed and pressure of life, demands that we master our inner world first, which can then act as a guide in navigating the complexities we deal with on a daily basis. The reason for this is that the physical world is always changing, no moment is like the last and the context and circumstances are always on the move. Our mind tends to follow it, create stories around it and draw natural conclusions based on the evidence we created from our previous observed experience. This has become a recipe for disaster, a recipe for a highly stressful and tumultuous life.

Noise, Movement, Drama

Stillness = Perspective

Without stillness we only experience the
noise movement and drama which is suffering.

In an effort to protect the boxes we believe we need to tick off in order to be successful, we can become boring and non-expansive. We close in, protect our 'stuff' and also forget to move.

The Social Requirements of Ticking the Right Boxes in Life

*Sitting just below the surface of our stressful
lives is a force that can assist us in everything we do.
The conscious realisation and integration of this
force is what I call, 'ultimate perception'.*

In October 2006, five Amish girls were murdered by a local milk delivery man named Charles Roberts. He killed them, and injured five more in a tiny, one-roomed schoolhouse in the town of Nickel Mines, Pennsylvania before turning the gun on himself. "There was not one desk, not one chair in the whole schoolroom that was not splattered with either blood or glass. There were bullet holes everywhere," said Deputy Coroner Janice Ballenger.

The way in which the Amish people responded to this situation was considered to be truly radical: they unconditionally forgave the killer. They refused to speak badly of him or to denigrate his character. They reached out to his family as fellow victims; they even designated a portion of the funds that poured in from around the world to the widow and the children of the shooter. After all, they were victims too, as far as they were concerned.

For many of us, automatic resistance and hatred are the only option we can see in such a situation. Take the test, put yourself in their shoes—how would you have reacted?

Let me ask you this… is such a radical departure from conventional behaviour *more*, or *less*, in alignment with who we really are? Our perceptions of virtually all situations are automatic; our mind makes a judgement and that becomes our truth. 'Can we really choose our perception and responses, or is automatic resistance to the pain we experience our only option?' The Amish response to the school shooting makes us stop and think about this doesn't it?

That happened in a land far away from where I grew up and continue to live a happy life. And perhaps the distance and environment make us different? Let's explore that a little.

What does it mean to be Australian?

Australians are known around the world as being happy-go-lucky, compassionate, having a good sense of humor, being able to 'do a deal on a handshake'; I've also heard that concept called the John Wayne handshake in the United States, but I prefer to call it the Kangaroo Paw handshake. Of course, you can never generalise but I think Australians as whole tend to be a nation that cares. We are generally an optimistic bunch, blessed with many natural resources and wonders, despite living in a particularly harsh land.

I feel very privileged to have grown up in Australia and am certain that this country can lead the way for positive change in the world. Australia is in a unique position as a young, wealthy, moderate and tolerant nation. We can be the creator of a new paradigm that moves away from a fear-based decision-making society to a society based more on authentic Love, starting with Love of Self where all love must start.

Interestingly the dark side of Australia is that it has the highest suicide rate of any country in the world. Some relevant statistics worth noting are that in 2021, 703,000 people around the world killed themselves, and an estimated 20 people for each one of those, considered or attempted it. By 2021, the highest number of deaths by suicide was in: New South Wales (880), followed by Queensland (783), Victoria (675), Western Australia (389) and South Australia (226). That's nearly 3,000 people. An average of nine deaths per day, and 75.9% of these are men.

How can this be?

What is it that triggers suicide of such proportions in 'the lucky country'?

Perhaps in some instances our self-loathing is so overwhelming that we go the extent of taking our own life. But why is that? Are we so busy looking outwardly for validation as to who we are as individuals that we have en masse, lost our ability to find inner peace? Perhaps we're so busy looking outwards for personal satisfaction and happiness that we forget that fulfilment start from the inside and radiates out.

In 2023, in Australia and in many other countries, everywhere we look advertising tells us that we'll "be happy when" we own something, go somewhere, do something, have a something. Is that reality? We fall into the trap of beating ourselves up when we don't achieve, have, be, or do something, which is all about what I call above the line thinking. That's about ticking boxes and thinking we will get clarity, satisfaction, - even love - from external sources.

As a nation we have never believed that we *couldn't* punch above our weight in anything! So, we excelled in sport, business, entertaining and the arts, standards of living, and economic management. From businesspeople to farmers and tradespeople, we are known globally as incredibly hard workers. This is depicted in films, historical stories of survival, while anyone who goes on a 'Rite of Passage OE', (overseas adventure typically undertaken between 18 – 25 for at least 6 months or longer) will soon learn that getting work as an Aussie is easy because of that reputation for our having a great work ethic.

For 30 plus years I have been on a journey to better understand myself and others. From the age of 16 I suffered terrible acne on my face, back and chest. I was one of the first people in Australia to be put on the powerful drug Roaccutane for my severe acne condition. The low self-esteem and lack of confidence that ensued, set me on a journey. That journey involved deep exploration of inner and outer worlds.

I learned to tick a lot of boxes early in my life. My outer world has consisted predominantly of business pursuits, mixed with family and a variety of passions including surfing, yoga, meditation, cycling, spiritual and personal development. At the age of 22, after completing a university degree, (I was told it would be good for me) I started my first business called *Listen Clothing* based on producing a series of prints and fashion garments which promoted environmental messages in a tasteful and non-confrontational way. I've since also created and achieved many things with my other businesses that I'm proud of, and like my father before me, I am blessed with strong entrepreneurial spirit and abilities.

The Game of Resistance

I have always had a passion for personal and spiritual development and for deep inquiry into the truth of what makes us tick (The inner world). In many ways this has been a much more exciting and rewarding exploration than my business achievements. I have experienced many different types of healing, including meditation, yoga and spiritual exploration and discovering the inner world continues to be a huge part of my life and who I see myself to be. I discovered that the so-called spiritual world that I was looking for and approaching in much the same way as I approached business and the other achievements in my life was in fact, not attainable in the same way.

I discovered that there was actually nothing to attain at all. Still, I tried and strained and struggled, always trying to get to a place more comfortable and less painful than the place I had found myself in at any given moment. I did this over and over again until I could do it no more. Finally, this is when a new journey began, one of acceptance, full experience, inner integrity and a knowing that, and understanding that, life is not always about feeling 'good'. Instead, I came to learn that mastery lay in accepting, maybe even looking forward to, feeling bad, so that I could recognise the stressful thinking behind this and get back on track.

I learned that resistance to the reality of any situation never helped resolve anything, yet I could feel nothing but resistance for long stretches of both my working life and my relationship with my wife of 30 years. In my struggle, I kept looking for relief by changing my thinking and resistance levels to any given situation. I also began to see how as a society we had bought into the idea that we need fear and stress to motivate and drive us. I found many great teachers along the way that have helped me build clarity, learn insights and discover the wonder of who I really am.

This book is my way of sharing with you, if you are walking a similar pathway of yearning to learn these things, what my journey has been, and how it's unfolded to help me sometimes experience a state of Is-ness and when I'm not experiencing that connected state how to remember and remind myself it is the Truth nonetheless. The sun is always present, we are that Sun, when clouds come, we can no longer see the sun but we are still the sun nonetheless.

How do we wake up?

How do we get in touch with our nature and act from that place? This is not about being a goody-two-shoes, it's about being real, calling it and feeling it and resolving it internally. Un-tying our inner turmoil and then acting from that empowered perspective. This is not a job for the faint hearted. Sure, we could all feel good, hold hands and sing Kumbaya but that ain't Love. So, what is it, and why should you give a damn?

How *do* we **find** Love?

How do we **discover** who we are?

Where do we look?

Is there a special way to **approach** it?

What will it be as it **unfolds and reveals** itself?

This book takes you by the hand and gives you the model that will explain how to be more fulfilled, enriched and empowered and then show you how to use this to achieve what you want in the world. And as we consider the mindset of the victims in the Amish shooting, their response, and the actions they took, maybe some of this will start to make a lot more sense.

Are you ready to explore who you are when your stressful thoughts are un-tied, and you are looking forward to whatever is presented because you are not fighting with life anymore?

This is the real secret to how we can transform ourselves and subsequently our family, neighborhood, planet, galaxy, universe and beyond. It is my hope that you will soon realise that you don't need the carrot and the stick to take action!

Living Above and Below the Line - The New Paradigms

The biggest obstacle to a great life

is a good life!

We've probably all heard the concept of the iceberg – where we are reminded that the real size of an iceberg is far more significant below the surface of the water line that what we see above. Using this as an analogy I want to guide you towards understanding the simple above and below aspects of our lives.

I have briefly touched on my interpretation of our human needs to go through life ticking various boxes to adhere to societal expectations, and when we are out there 'doing our thing.' What we show of ourselves, our intentions to 'do what's right' and 'make our parents proud' are examples of doing what is our 'above the line' version of living.

Let's consider an alternative model to the concept of icebergs that I believe reflects the real power of what goes on above the line and below the line. I'd like to introduce to you the Amped Stillness model.

Introducing the Amped Stillness Model

We live most of our lives above the line, ticking boxes and getting things done. It feels good to achieve a goal and get things done but if that's all we do, our lives can become shallow and meaningless. In the Amped Stillness model, the top part of the triangle represents the boxes we tick and how in the process we become more certain and rigid in our thinking, beliefs and stories we tell ourselves about the way things are. Having ticked off so many of our boxes, we think of ourselves as having grown up. We have. But we have also 'grown in'.

In the process of 'growing up and in', we leave no space for new ideas or thinking and are arguably very set in our ways!

Some would argue teenagers are the same way. I recently saw a bumper sticker which read – *Teenagers: move out of home, get a job, earn 100's of 1000's of dollars now while you still know everything.*

Once jammed into the top part of the triangle we are increasingly certain that it is our stories, based on our successes and failures, which define us. It not until some of our ticked boxes fail or fall apart that we wake up to the realisation there might be more to this thing we call Life.

Above the line is movement – chaos, uncertainty, boxes to tick, expectations of ourselves and others in our lives.

Below the line is Stillness, which is intelligent, blissful, and True.

Stillness *vs* Movement

All of us are living our lives constantly both above and below the line. Stillness (below the line) is accessed simply by being aware of our own Awareness.

Stillness gives us the opportunity to look back at all the movement going on in our life. We can only see the movement, drama and chaos created by our stories when we experience Stillness. However, we can't experience   Stillness while we are consumed by movement and distraction.

The ground rules for operation above the line and below the line are different. The things we learn and become competent in help define our above the line story and how we're seen in the world whereas below the line we are tasked with unlearning and letting go of all the techniques that seem to work above the line. Once we experience Stillness through letting go and personal diminishment and detachment, we direct that Awareness to the things we want to achieve in the world. Without awareness of our inherent Stillness, we are always navigating life from perspective that is moving and changing.

Discovering Stillness may not be a straight line, which is why we need courage to face our fears to accept that continual movement. Striving does not hold the answer - contrary to what we had always thought. The breaking down of the old Amped way of doing things in favour of a more integrated approach may be difficult at first.

The constant transitioning between both the moving (Amped), achievement-driven self and the Stillness we are is represented by the figure of eight or infinity sign which signifies that at any time we have the capacity to live life from a more balanced perspective. We experience life from the new perspective which is Still and True. This is about integration instead of constantly transitioning from one side to the other.

So, we learn to integrate the movement (Amped) and the Awareness (Stillness) in our life.

Introducing the AMPED Stillness Model

Above the line is about ticking those boxes that other people and society in general use to indicate success and achievement. That's about achieving, being, doing, and having things. Below the line represents Stillness, infinite possibilities, a state of Being.

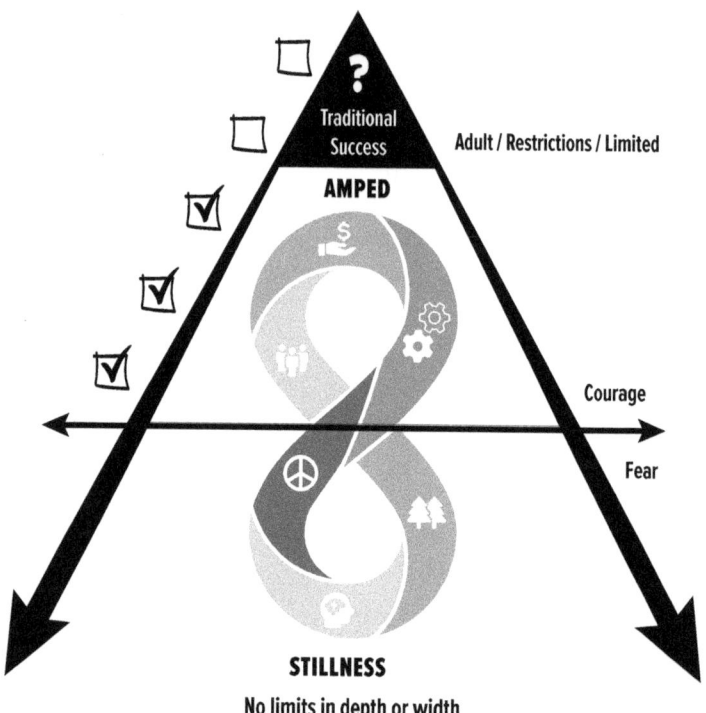

Our path to achievement is therefore sometimes quite predictable depending on our socio-economic and demographic circumstances.

For me it looked something like this; each achievement representing a ticked box up the left side of the above the line triangle.

- ☑ Finishing school
- ☑ Gained entrance to university
- ☑ Graduated
- ☑ Started my first business
- ☑ Sold business
- ☑ Got married
- ☑ Started second business
- ☑ Had first child
- ☑ Sold second business
- ☑ Had more children
- ☑ Bought a house
- ☑ Bought a holiday house
- ☑ Etc etc…

Does some of that look familar to you too?

Obviously, there are many things you could call box-ticking. Even on a daily basis we are building our stories and concepts about what the world is and who we are, often the ideals of others handed down through many generations. Our DNA stores memories and without Awareness we simply live out those memories.

One of the main ways we see ourselves in the world is through our professions. When we give someone our business card it does not say that we are a father or a mother, it does not declare what our most adventurous experiences have been or what we are most passionate about in life. Instead, it says what we DO… and every other concept, story and idea hangs off that. For example, our professions can dictate our lives by determining with reasonable accuracy where our kids go to school, what holidays we go on, what suburbs we live in, what our kids get for Christmas etc. Whilst we don't often think or reflect in these terms, vocation is incredibly powerful in terms of how we see ourselves and for this reason, it is where we are the most vulnerable.

Do you know people who are perhaps lawyers and doctors, accountants or engineers who do not know how to let go of that role regardless of their circumstances? Not all professional success stories are paved with people happy with their chosen profession/career/job.

Our professional roles can be so powerful they colour everything we do and how we see the world – and how the world sees us. But when we are truly passionate about what we do, the role seems to become particularly merged in our Psyche and we lose track of time and immerse ourselves in a given experience. This merging of what we do with who we are is a huge clue in the roles in our life. Rather than separate us from ourselves, our roles are there to serve us to fully understand, paradoxically, who we are beyond them. Some people might refer to this as a Flow State, which is the integration of what we do with who we are.

So What?!

Roles, stories, concepts and ideas become our identity, they color everything we see out there, whether we are conscious of it or not.

For each of us, our own story which starts from birth and develops very strongly in the first five years of our lives, sets our respective moulds. We see life in a certain way, then once we have ticked specific boxes (based on family, societal, and individual expectations), we start to develop a lot of very good strategies for protecting ourselves from any wounds gathered along the way. All of that continues to shape us from cradle to grave.

The ground rules for living above the line are essentially that everyone has a job to do. Just as it is a teacher's job to teach our children, so it is a surgeon's job to perform operations, but these are jobs of profession. There are many other additional types of jobs that push our buttons on a daily basis. For example, it our parents' job to encourage us or dissuade us from taking risks, our partner's job to ensure the trash is out or the social invitations are responded to. But let's take that one step further, because it might also be a business partner's job to betray us by embezzling our funds, for a spouse to cheat on us, or for a friend to disappoint us - all to help us further work out who we really are and how we are continuing to find ourselves among the many ups and downs in our lives.

This may all sound a bit bizarre, but the point is that shit happens, doesn't it? Yet most of the time we resist what has happened to us and pile more on top of what's there. We place the shit of resistance on top of the shit of reality. If we can learn to accept that when people perform their jobs of betrayal, mistrust and disappointment we have a choice, much the same as the Amish demonstrated after the school shooting, I referred to earlier, and their thinking that their actions around forgiveness would make it better.

This is not about inaction.

The ground rules require us to get very clear and deal with our emotions and wounding for any given challenge and then move forward. Of course, this is not a perfect world, and I am not suggesting that all this takes place in some sterile container, but I propose that a state of Awareness is something that can help us *fully feel* into and better assess any given situation.

Life above the line is a great thing once we get the ground rules down but so few of us even have these ground rules. In fact, most of us aren't even aware that we are in pain, because we define ourselves by our profession, roles, or our personality, but as we're beginning to understand perhaps, we are more than that.

The Navaho Native Americans always weave what they call a spirit line into their beautifully colorful rugs. The spirit line is an intentional imperfection in the rug which acknowledges our inherent imperfections as human beings. It recognises that we are wounded and *that is where our real potential lays.* We as westerners, on the other hand, want to keep our imperfections hidden from the world. Imperfections are perceived as undesirable and bad. Society tells us we should do everything in our power to hide our undesirable parts from the world, so we push those parts that hurt the most even further down. We develop increasingly clever strategies to keep people away from knowing that part of ourselves. This can be at both a physical and psychological level.

Only when we recognise the reality of a situation and then we become aware of what is really happening in our lives - and are prepared to face it, or even just see it - do we have a chance to respond effectively. The ground rules above the line always lie in awareness, openness and honesty with self. (Inner integrity).

It comes down to choices!

What are the above the line habits you can choose to give you what you really want? Do you know what you really want? The above the line world is a reflection of the things you have acquired and done to get you to where you think you want to be. We all acquire and do things (tick boxes in the name of happiness) but when we look at our lives above the line it's easy to come to the conclusion that there is perhaps a more direct route to happiness.

Gratitude is a great habit to practice. Being actively grateful for all that you do and don't have in your life. I know how hard it is to find gratitude in times of challenge, but being grateful teaches us to focus in on high vibrations, for gratitude is one of the highest vibrational states of all. According to David Hawkins in his brilliant book the Eye of the I[2], the highest vibrational state is Love and the lowest is Shame. David created a scale from 0 (lowest) to 1000 (highest) vibration and used kinesiology (a method with a high level of scientific rigor) to determine the vibrational integrity of everything from companies to countries to books and films. This was a fascinating study which makes us realise that everything has a vibration which can be tangibly measured.

What are you doing above the line to optimise your vibration in the name of happiness, health and awareness?

---

2   Eye of the I, by David Hawkins, Hay House, 2013

Focusing on high vibrational thoughts such as Love, Gratitude, Hope, Trust and so on are a great start. Your conveyor belt may be moving so quickly that at first this seems incredibly challenging but never give up on your quest. There are many techniques that you can use to untie the resistance that exists in your world. In fact, some of these techniques are so powerful and effective that you may soon find yourself being grateful for challenges that arise, because they provide the opportunity to deal with them in more in depth and growth-focused ways. Once they are dealt with you will feel a greater sense of freedom and that feels good!!!

I'd like to go back to the concept of *Below* the Line Living and how to integrate these two parts of your life – the above and below the line parts - so you have a full understanding of where practicality and spirituality meet and integrate into your whole life.

Many great authors have written about this in a variety of ways, but I'd like to explore with you how to interpret and then integrate this as part of being both *spiritual* and *human*. It's about the way in which we accept that our physical, emotional, and mental selves have needs, wants, and are frail and imperfect, but that we are also spiritual beings having human experiences in order to expand who we are, both above and below the line. It's about spirituality and practicality and where they need to meet to ensure that we have a whole of life experience.

The Integration

Having begun to see the dualistic way I was approaching the world - Amped achievement on one side and Stillness or Beingness on the other side - it occurred to me that without the existence of the Being, there were no roles, achievements or life story. How then can we be conscious of who we are, achieve what we want to achieve, and fully engage in playing the game of life.

When I began to play with the integration of achievement and

Beingness I found they worked very well together. Conscious exploration and experience of the inner world through fully feeling any given situation helped open the way for a cognitive change in perception. (Just trying to simplify this sentence) I found I didn't need to be searching for problems and digging into my past, because life presented me with all the resistance I wanted to play with. I started looking forward to resistance so that I could consciously untie (or prefer un-tie?) what was standing in my way. It became like a game. The fear of being vulnerable began to drop away and the Truth became my highest priority i.e. the Truth of what I was feeling or the reality of the situation.

I also have a passion for writing and communication. I love business and I love personal exploration in the areas of health, wealth and wisdom, all of which are vital to thriving in today's world now more than ever. We are at a critical point in history where we really do need to be the change we want to see in the world. We can no longer wait to be led. As much as we would like to believe that some superhero or brilliant political figure is going to save us it is clear that he or she is not. We must therefore learn to understand ourselves at a very deep and fundamental level. It is no longer a luxury; it is essential for us as a species.

The Concept of the Box

*Wanting certainty is an obstacle
to happiness.*

When setting out on this journey of writing a book I knew some of the content was going to be challenging to communicate. My book coach Dixie encouraged me to introduce you the reader into the more challenging principles of this book clearly and gently. And it's important we make some distinctions early about where this is going to take you. As a result, we developed this model called The Box, which serves as a metaphor for our ultimate journey to freedom and consciousness.

There are many types of boxes; some we drive, we eat from, and those we live in etc. And then there are the many boxes we tick, which also tend to be the same boxes we define ourselves by.

For example, I passed my final school exams, and having ticked that box I gained entrance to university. After ticking that box, I got a job as an accountant. Then having ticked the career box I made enough money to buy a home, I got married and had kids etc. Our individual boxes combine to create the Story we call our life.

What's the number one question we are asked when first meeting someone at a dinner party? Yes, you guessed it... *"What do you do?*" We answer with the latest career box we have ticked and the listener in turn puts us in the box they associate with the answer based on their way of seeing the world.

Imagine if we instead were asked, 'how do you define yourself?'

The boxes we tick could be related to goals we have intentionally set for ourselves or things that just seemed to happen in our lives. The point is that society sees box-ticking as being all about Achievement or Results. All politicians and business leaders seem hell bent on ticking certain boxes as their way of showing the world they have done a good job.

It is worth noting that, in our culture, boxes can both be ticked or remain unticked. The ticked box is what we call success and the unticked box we typically think of as failure. However, success can lead to failure and failure can lead to success, can't it? The story below illustrates this point. We never really know until later whether the boxes we tick will actually lead to so called positive or negative outcomes.

There's a Taoist parable called *Sāi Wēng Lost His Horse* about a poor Chinese farmer. It goes something like this:

A farmer and his son had a beloved horse who helped the family earn a living. One day, the horse ran away, and their neighbours exclaimed, "Your horse ran away, what terrible luck!" The farmer replied, "Maybe so, maybe not."

A few days later, the horse returned home, leading a few wild horses back to the farm as well. The neighbours shouted out, "Your horse has returned, and brought several horses home with him. What great luck!" The farmer replied, "Maybe so, maybe not."

Later that week, the farmer's son was trying to break in one of the horses and she threw him to the ground, breaking his leg. The neighbours cried, "Your son broke his leg, what terrible luck!" The farmer replied, "Maybe so, maybe not."

A few weeks later, soldiers from the national army marched through town, recruiting all the young men of the village for the army. They did not take the farmer's son, because he had a broken leg. The neighbours shouted, "Your boy is spared, what tremendous luck!" To which the farmer replied, "Maybe so, maybe not. We'll see."

People in China have long held the story as a means of reminding people when something bad happens, there may be a silver lining and will say: "Sai Weng Shi Ma" - which translates to: *Remember the old man and his horse.*

We are sense-making machines, so we use our stories in relation to our boxes. Those same stories create a self-justifying loop which consolidates our newly and or long held view of the world. The farmer in the story above was a very wise man who knew that life is perpetual, and the circumstances are ever-changing. What appears fortuitous in one moment can easily turn out to be not good in the next. Most of our stories are on a perpetual loop I call the conveyor belt.

Over time the boxes we tick tend to define how we see ourselves in the world and how the world defines us. Have you ever observed how a doctor gets treated in a social situation versus a truck driver?

Imagine a very large box into which all our achievements and failures are placed and then mix that with corresponding stories and emotions. It creates our unique personalities over time and much of this is cemented in early childhood and adolescence. We define ourselves by our stories such as – I'm bold/shy or generous/tight, sensitive/thick skinned, mad, happy, sad and so on depending on our circumstances. Our stories are created from our experiences, and are created consciously, subconsciously and unconsciously in order to avoid fear, seek love, or impress someone. And always in our mind our stories can be justified by other stories that support what we can see and experience in the world.

Understand this:
Our stories are always relative truths based on our perceptions, and they rule our world.

Of course, within the box there are many stories and traits we are not aware of, and they also determine our actions. This box-ticking seems to work quite well for a good portion of our life but for many of us (arguably all of us) there comes a time when we start to question how well this works. The questions usually arise at a time of crisis during which the boxes we have ticked no longer make sense. For example, you might have poured your heart, soul and time into a relationship and your partner comes home one night and tells you that it's over. You may have worked tirelessly on a business and your business partner declares they no longer value your contribution and want to make drastic changes. At these times life as we know it makes no sense. Our boxes implode in confusion. We try desperately to piece the box back together but find it's smashed into a million pieces. Where to start?

Once we've pulled ourselves back together, we go on to create new boxes and stories to explain our new predicament and history.

There is a phenomenon that happens with athletes post an Olympic Games' four-year cycle where successful athletes often fall into a deep depression because the boxes that they have been striving to tick have been ticked and no longer exist.

It is human nature to strive and tick boxes and when our boxes are taken away our psyche is forced to make sense of life through a different pathway which does not currently exist.

Box-ticking seems to be an important part of life for our own sense of achievement and making sense of the world, but it has its limits. We will explore these limits later in the book.

Can you Change your box?

The boxes we tick become the substance of our life. The biggest box contains our unique stories. Think of this as being like the vessel we take through our lives. We all process these achievements differently based on many things, including our respective upbringing, our environment and aspects of Self which is 'unknown'.

It's easy to see personalities and behaviours from a very young age, whether in your own children or their friends. They display traits which are inexplicable at times, and not always evidently based on nature or nurture. There may be an innate shyness or outgoingness for some, some kids can be exhibitionists while others are recluses, some are warriors, others are lovers or nurturers. These traits and 'ways of being' are a mystery in many respects as the qualities seem to be innate and not always learned from any type of conditioning from life's experiences or environment. For example, even a set of twins might be completely different from each other in terms of personality; boldness versus withdrawn, courage in the face of adversity or persuasiveness versus ability to blend in with their peers.

To some extent we come into this world pre-programmed. We each have our various gifts and challenges. My three kids all have different gifts and challenges and if ever they have said or intimated a 'why me' (based on whatever was going on at the time) I'd simply tell them that 'we all have our crosses to bear'. One person may have acne, another may be short, another may not know how to express feelings, have health issues or challenges in relationships. I remind them that every person whether they show it or not, rich, poor or middle class, all have life lessons to overcome either internally or externally.

Think about a big steel box with a certain operating system contained within, which needs reverse engineering to understand its many chinks, edges and developmental scars. Just as we have our own parts of Self that make up The Box, it is that which we find most challenging that will provide us with either limits or grist for the mill. I've lost count of how many successful people were told by their teachers that they would not amount to anything - a comment like this can seriously rattle anyone's ability to tick boxes (and often does). Or for some people, such a comment can also be the stick that drives you to tick boxes of achievement, and maybe even over-compensate. The reverse engineering of our Big Box to discover its Nature (which is our True Nature) is in many ways what we call Life.

Some Boxes (people) seem to know what they want from early adulthood or before. I was recently reading about Oscar Piastri, who from childhood dreamed of being a Formula 1 driver and moved steadily through the ranks to achieve his goal. Of course, there was never a guarantee he was going to make it to the levels he has so far, but the point is he knew without doubt what the major box was he wanted to tick. This box now defines his life above anything else so far. It is true, and maybe stating the obvious, to say that the fastest way between two points is a straight line and some of us are fortunate enough to know, early in our lives, which line we wish to take. The destination is clear to us from childhood.

It may seem at times that greatness also has its own spectacularly high sets of challenges. Maybe the personalities that are required to achieve outstanding levels of success in the first place are balanced differently. For example, Michael Jackson, for all his extraordinary levels of talent, rose to the greatest heights but also fell to great depths at the end of his life.

Is it possible that what is required to achieve that level of success in the first place means that one box within the Big Box consumed all the focus. Whilst we inevitably get name and fame from this approach it seems to create problems and imbalance.

It's perhaps fair to say that while fame is an ultimate attraction for many, it's not always what turns out to be the most attractive thing about ticking a box. Fame in itself, is not always all it is cracked up to be, is a line that has been repeated by many a superstar over the years.

When I was younger, I was always in such a hurry to get to places. I was also very altruistic about what my box's path should be and struggled to find what really suited it. Having fun and ticking boxes is not enough for some and for others it's just fine.

If you are happy just living this life and not asking a lot of questions, then you might be on the right track. Alternatively, you could just be resigned to the fact that this is the way life is and have developed a good resistance to suffering the day-to-day grind. I am in some ways envious of boxes which can move in a straight line with complete focus and concentration. For some Boxes, growing and expanding is imperative and for others it is an unnecessary inconvenience. The irony is that the Truth is ultimately realised with focus, attention, and faith.

My wife who is an executive coach facilitates a personality profiling tool called PRINT® which identifies from nine different options what our key drivers are and what makes us tick. I score as 4/7 which means I am looking for purpose and meaning (in life) and having fun (this actually explains a lot about my life and how it has played out). What I find particularly fascinating is that this PRINT® tool tells us that the modus operandi of our individual Boxes is all created by the age of 15.

My Box has been down many rabbit holes looking for the Ultimate Solution. Those solutions have taken many forms – small business, franchising, public companies, technologies, startups, bullion, property developing, consulting, company directorships, investing in equities, diet, health, long distance running, swimming and cycling, surfing, yoga and spirituality. Some boxes are on a perpetual journey for me to find the holy grail of discovering we are The Box, not the boxes we tick or don't tick.

Every box pursued and ticked fills our Big Boxes with an identity and reason for being. We are judged by the outside world on how well we each tick our boxes. We stand and observe others and perceive that he/she was a success or failure based on what boxes they may have ticked off, and therefore their possessions, career, family, relationships and so on. We create stories and beliefs which become part of our subconscious.

However, it needs to be said that the contents of our Big Boxes are always changing and moving. They are dynamic and those moving parts are relative in nature, meaning they can be judged by ourselves and others as good or bad, a success or failure depending on who's looking at them and through what lens. Our personal values and priorities usually determine how well we've done. But those values are set by a box outside of ourselves which has an interest in us thinking and feeling a certain way. I'm thinking of marketing and big business which has an interest - for the sake of their profits - in the way we think and act.

IDENTITY
'We ARE the BOX'

We go from identifying with the boxes we tick, to becoming aware that 'I am the Big box'. We then experience life as spacious and free.

We need to unpack our Big Box to discover its True nature. We unpack our box though awareness and watching that which we think, feel and do. We watch the contents of our Big Box and this in turn leads to something miraculous as we discover we are not the contents of our Box. Let me say that again - We are not the contents of our Box. We are the Box.

By watching the contents of our Box we begin to realise what we are not the boxes and in doing so we move closer to realising who we truly are. We are the Big Box – the Box is us.

We are not the contents of our Box. We are that which exists before the boxes that seem to define us are ticked. i.e. We are the Big Box.

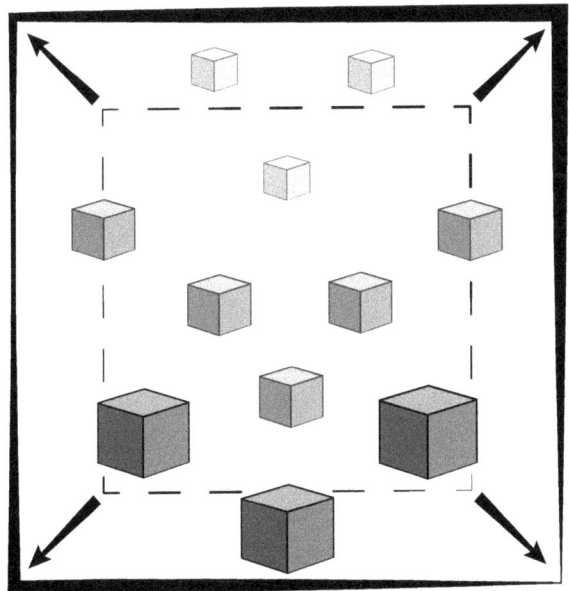

As the Big Box expands and becomes more of the lived experience, the little boxes become less important - we call this detachment.

What Do We Put in and Take Out of our Boxes?

*Personal diminishment is just as
important as personal development.*

When we come into this world, we are essentially an Empty Box full of potential and hope. We start out fine and then start to "de-fine ourselves", only to then re-fine ourselves.

As we set out on our life's journey, sometimes consciously, but usually unconsciously, we pursue what we think will make us happy. Society is constantly reinforcing the belief in us that Happiness is "out there" in the things we achieve, what we acquire and the quality of our relationships.

As an animal we are more advanced than most which is both our great *fortune* and *misfortune*. Our advanced intelligence allows us freedom of choices and to be masters of our destiny, but it is also our *mis*fortune *because* it gives us choice and allows us to be masters of our own destiny.

There are so many messages out there in real life telling us how to eat, how to look, what to own, how to be great in relationships etc. How can we possibly know what we should do and where it's going to take us - when what we see and hear is so relentlessly filled with mixed messages? We can model successful people, and this seems like a great idea until we realise that those apparent icons of success are not us. They each have completely different skill sets, belief systems, backgrounds, and desires or fears than we do. Of course, there are general things that we can each do to improve our personal existences, and that extends into community improvements too. Success does indeed leave clues and that is how we advance as a civilisation.

Back to you (personally), however, and the question of what boxes are you going to tick to make your life meaningful day to day? Is it important to you that you leave a legacy you can be proud of? We are driven by such ideals but also much more primary and often unconscious needs or instincts.

The Primary Needs of Certainty and Significance

We all want to be sure we can pay next month's rents or mortgages and to know that we are valued in our work, family life and by our peers. Not ticking both these boxes can leave us feeling scared and angry. So, it's only natural that we go out into the world and achieve things that help us feel more significant and/or give us more certainty. But it's not that simple, because we also need some degree of uncertainty. This is based on the concept that if we woke up every morning knowing that every day was going to be exactly like the last it would be a pretty dull life wouldn't it?

You may think that long periods of peace and tranquillity sound like a blissful way to live, but to not have the seasons change, or the people around us grow and develop, or the chance of a holiday would be pushing our respective tolerance levels. We crave change when we don't have it… just think about the last time it didn't rain for a month, or the rain didn't stop for days on end.

Life above the line is so complex because there are so many moving parts. How in the world do we keep everything in balance and keep ourselves and our relationships happy, walking the line between certainty and uncertainty? The short answer is we can't! But despite this we stay on the conveyor belt doing the things we know, and that which make us comfortable. Most of us tick boxes that give us more certainty or more significance and we occasionally mix things up a bit. Of course, there are exceptions to this, but bear with me for now.

For many years I practised yoga and then I discovered a love for cycling. I ticked a number of boxes in cycling, including riding 320kms in a day to raise money for charity. Yoga gradually disappeared from my life as cycling was then ticking all my 'needs' boxes. My need for significance was met through my cycling, better than it had been by yoga. (Who doesn't feel significant in Lycra?! Haha.) For example, there were friends telling me I rode well etc, and there was certainty from knowing that I'd feel great after the ride with a post endorphin rush. Then there's the uncertainty that comes with understanding that cycling is a dangerous sport. We ride around the streets with very little protection with the very real possibility of being hit by a car or clipping the wheel of a fellow rider in front of you and coming down hard. Cycling (for me) has it all! However, while I was well and truly ticking the box and feeling great, my hamstrings were getting tighter and tighter until my back was so painful, I could hardly walk. The Yoga box had been moved to one side to make way for the cycling box which I was ticking every which way. Perhaps the yoga still needed to be part of my overall box-ticking after all?

I tell this story to demonstrate that life is dynamic and ever changing. What is a good box to tick today, may need reassessment tomorrow.

Having said that, one of the keys to success above the line is 'stick-to-it-ness'.

I started *The Tap Doctor* with my partner Archie Gubbins in 1994. We turned it into a franchise business and started selling franchises after I read the book *The E Myth* by Michael Gerber[3] I remember wondering 'if this stuff really works' and then found a business I could apply the principles to. After several years we had 20 vans running around Perth and other parts of Australia. There was one problem – I got bored! After surviving the many challenges most startups face, we had some momentum, a well-respected brand and the business was making pretty good money, but it wasn't quick enough for me. I saw the money that could be made in stockbroking through my brother who was a stockbroker, and I had been brought up around talk of publicly listed companies due to my father being a very passionate investor and founder of several public companies. This was getting me far more excited than plumbing and franchising.

I went from working in *The Tap Doctor* business to becoming an investor in *The Tap Doctor* hoping that the business would be able to pay me dividends on top of the wage and commissions I was making as a stockbroker. Suffice to say I ended up selling my share of *The Tap Doctor* for what seemed like quite a lot of money at the time. Some years later that business has continued to grow and thrive, and I often feel I should have hung in there. At those times, little things like an unhappy franchisee for example seemed bigger than they actually were. I have since realised in many of the businesses that I have been involved in, you are often more resilient than you think you are.

Stockbroking was that bright shiny object that seemed logical to pursue at the time. However, despite my early enthusiasm, I soon got bored with sitting in front of a screen every day and quit after about 18 months.

Many of us tick the boxes that we think will give us significance, certainty and perhaps a dollop of uncertainty/challenge. We are constantly adjusting our boxes to be more optimal and better fall in line with these core needs, and much of this is done in a very unconscious way with no real understanding of what the end result will look like.

---

3   The EMyth Revisited, Michael Gerber, Harper Collins Revised Edition 2004

Many of my so called very (financially) successful friends have struck on the notion of being in pursuit of success their whole working life. This can be through the need for certainty or because they found their thing early and just kept doing it because they didn't run out of passion for it.

Our pursuit of new boxes seems like the main game at the time, everything seems to be riding on the boxes we tick. The things we achieve come to equate significantly with who we become. At least that's how it appears at the time. But as time passes, many of us do come to a point of questioning this very thing.

Is it enough?

Is there more?

What am I missing?

Box Failure

The challenge ultimately is that our boxes always fail sooner or later. Our health box gets sick or hurts itself; our business box(es) terminates or our relationship box(es) fail. Sooner or later in some form **we are going to have to confront Box Failure**. This does not mean we should not value the boxes we ticked so far. Of course, we should. After all, it was effective at defining how the world viewed us, and to a large extent how we defined ourselves. But I'm just saying be aware of your boxes and what they mean to you.

Resilience is about being able to deal with Box Failure. Whether it be voluntarily or involuntary, to have it exterminated, terminated or done with. Where does resilience really come from and how is it built or discovered? This is what we will look at in future chapters.

My Own Boxes

Many of us live a very convoluted life, until we don't.

I know I have been down many rabbit holes looking for what works best for me whether it be diet, occupation, sport, spirituality, investment, relationship, charity and so on. Maybe I've been looking for Nirvana! The realisation now is that I'm so grateful for all the times I've felt like I was knocking my head against brick walls as painful as that was. Little did I know at those times, it was perfect and necessary for me.

I think all our boxes are ultimately perfect and necessary for us all. How can they not be?

Let me explain that further. It's our own life and our experience to make sense of or not. Nothing we experience can be a waste or irrelevant if it moves us forward in some way to a new awareness, opportunity, realisation, or crossroads. Perhaps this will become clearer later in the book, but for now just feel into it and ask yourself this important question: would you really prefer to be someone else despite all your challenges and circumstances?

As I am fond of saying, the quickest way between two points is in a straight line but my life has been anything but that. I do know a lot of people who go in straight lines without being tempted by the new shiny objects on their horizon. And I have learned a lot from these types of people in recent times as very little is achieved without stick-to-it-ness. I've had to learn to see things through to maturity and all the uncertainty that also comes with that. The old Clash song 'Should I stay or should I go?' now says it best! I've got to say I am very grateful for my twists and turns in life. Those are the things that make us who we are. This is particularly the case when things don't work out as planned.

What doesn't kill me makes me stronger perhaps.

When I dug deep into what creates a successful life above the line, I noticed some very basic things about people who achieved the most in the world. They all had a basic level of practice they unknowingly adopted as part of their success rules.

I called them the 4 Buckets.

- Get Started
- Practise Routinely
- Never Give In
- Tick the Box

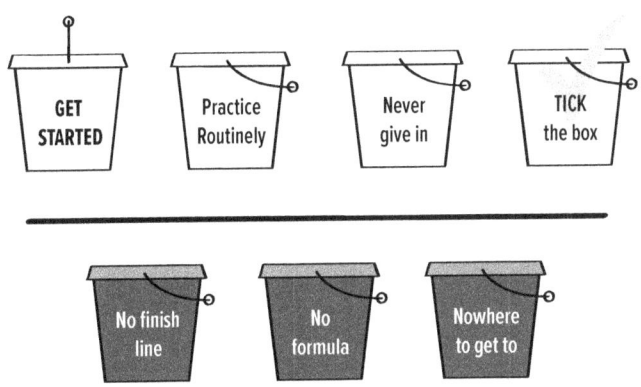

When practicing routinely, one should also note the concept of continual refinement. It's never going to be perfect from the get-go. Most things take time to develop and refine.

After returning to Perth from seven years living in the Southwest, we rented our home but I soon had enough of that and wanted to buy a house. However, it seemed impossible to find something in an acceptable price range in the suburb that my wife and I had our hearts set on. But I decided with a strong intent I was going to find a way.

I had met a residential property buying agent at a party a month earlier and had mentioned I was looking but said I would circle back when I had my finances in order. When I called her, she mentioned a property which had been on the market for a few months and was subdividable. I was immediately interested and asked if we could go through the property. I loved it but financing it was going to be tight; regardless I moved ahead as if it was done deal. My agent negotiated a great price on the property and there was a healthy profit if we could get the subdivision done in a particular way. I was able to purchase this subdividable property in a premium suburb with a loan from the bank, together with a higher interest personal loan at a time of record low interest rates; the planets aligned and what seemed like a dream became a reality.

What was in play here?

1. I got clear about what I wanted.

2. I imagined what I wanted.

3. I got emotionally involved and felt a passion for the purchase of the property.

4. I took action – finance was the big one, I used a trusted mortgage broker who helped me navigate that landscape.

5. I kept moving in the direction of my desired outcome no matter what.

6. I took action on a lot of fronts, just starting conversations with buyers, agents and mortgage brokers created momentum and information flow in the right direction.

7. As different, more and or better information came to hand I would act on it accordingly.

8. The outcome was very good from a financial perspective and allowed me to pay back some debt, make some investments and spoil me and my wife a little.

Of Life, Love, and Learning

*Don't wish it was easier, wish you
were better.*

In February 1989 I had just fallen in love with an English girl named Antonia who was on a world tour and had stopped through Yallingup where I was living at the time. After a month or so it was time for her to move on to Sydney for the next leg of her tour. I, of course decided I had to find a way to be with her, but I didn't want to chase her to be only motive (perhaps I needed an excuse). So, I found an intensive three-month addictions counselling course based on the 12 step Alcoholics Anonymous program used by the United States Navy to treat their addicted service men and women.

My plan was coming together nicely; the course started within three weeks of her arrival in Sydney, and it lasted for the duration of her stay there. I turned up in Sydney for the start of my course and the first thing I did was call her up excitedly to let her know I had arrived. To my absolute surprise, I quickly learned that she didn't want a bar of me. She had gone cold on the idea of our romance.

I remember feeling completely confused and angry with her response, so I persisted in reaching out to her, but after several days I was still getting the cold shoulder. I finally sat down with a good mate who was living in Sydney and explained to him that I didn't know what was happening or why and he just shrugged his shoulders and offered useful feedback such as maybe she's got another guy etc.

There was a whole new reality I quickly had to come to terms with. I had committed to a three-month intensive training process, but I would not be sharing my experience in Sydney with Antonia. I was just getting used to the idea of life without her when she reached out to me with a new attitude. I still couldn't tell you what happened to change her mind, but I have now been married to Antonia for more than 32 years and can say it has offered more growth to both of us than either of us could have imagined or at times wanted!!

We never know how our life is going to roll. The more easily we come to terms with our ever changing and new realities the happier we will be. Life tends to give us both what we want, and what we need, but first we have to recognise the resistance that leads to suffering.

After qualifying as a drug and alcohol counsellor I followed Antonia to her home in the United Kingdom and ended up in London where I got a job at a family drug and alcohol counselling hospital called Charter Knightingale, one of the most prestigious centres in Britain. My next job required a one-month long interview at another private treatment centre called Promis Hay Farm in Nonnington, Kent, where for four weeks I was required to experience what it was like to be on the receiving end of treatment with drug, alcohol, and food addicts.

As you can imagine, those in the treatment program had many stories to tell. Some were of crime, breaking the trust of their loved ones, losing jobs, relationships, money and everything in between. I quickly learned that despite the horror stories that led them to be in treatment, in their sober states while sharing those stories, each and every one was a sweet person, just simply doing their best.

There is nothing like addiction and its very predictable outcomes to highlight the contrast between who we are and how we act. I always felt great compassion for the person at the centre of the story in their sober state. To me it always seemed like there was such a wide gap between the actions taken and the sober awareness of that patient.

One patient was a top technical specialist in the music industry, working for some of the biggest bands in the world including Queen and Metallica. I shared a room with him the entire time I was there, during which he shared with me that he had murdered someone in a Cocaine-induced rage. I liked this man in his sober state and felt grateful that this was the only way I had to experience him.

When we are living our life through the many little boxes that fill our Big Box we are not seeing or experiencing the world as it is. We are experiencing it as we are. It is like looking at the world through a bespoke set of glasses that colours everything we see.

If we can know and experience ourselves as the box that contains all our stories, then there is no need to identify with this or that. Our boxes are not unimportant for they are the resume that contains our so-called successes, failures and the subsequent stories we have created around them. But as the addict in us makes clear, (I believe we are all addicts to greater or less extent) there is never any permanent satisfaction in achievement. Achievement of our small boxes are temporary, but our Big Box offers an opportunity for expansive knowing that all is perfect.

This is perfect. That is perfect. Take the perfect from the perfect and all that is left is perfect. The Perfect Prayer IIsha Upanishad

Later in the book we will explore the pristine untouchable nature of the box which contains all and is not separate from anything.

Ticking My Entrepreneurial Boxes

My company *Listen Clothing* was born from pure passion and entrepreneurial drive. I loved this as it was my first true business. My baby if you like. It is so satisfying to have now passed this on to my youngest son, 23-year-old Charlie, who is doing great things with a brand for which I maintained the trademark more than 35 years.

Like a lot of businesses, *Listen Clothing* started with one simple idea. I heard on the news that they there was pipeline running from Sydney to Bondi Beach pumping raw sewage into the ocean. This disturbed me greatly, but I also saw opportunity in this abhorrent situation. If you're a surfer, you'll know that the greatest surf break on the planet is called Banzai Pipeline. My vision was to use a play on words to make an environmental point. The caption for my T-shirt idea, which was the genesis of *Listen Clothing*, was Blind Mullets (which is an Aussie slang term for faeces) at Bondi Pipeline. The graphics were that of the said blind mullets surfing a cross-section of a concrete pipeline which formed the shape of a wave.

This was my golden ticket, or so I believed at the time. 'Everyone in Australia' was going to want one of these T-shirts and I would be rich! Needless to say, it didn't quite turn out that way, but this original idea spawned a bigger vision which became *Listen Clothing*.

After my years as a drug and alcohol counsellor and some of the early personal growth I had done, I sat down and reflected on a big question: what was the most important thing in life to me?

AWARENESS!

Big questions get big answers, and it still surprises me to this day that the answer stands as true for me now as it did then. Awareness was what I considered the most important thing in life at the age of 23 so I named my company *Aware Holdings Pty Ltd.*

To me Awareness is almost like a living entity in and of itself, and God knows I've wandered about a lot on my 35-year journey since then. But Awareness just sits there and laughs at my plans, waiting for me to come back and realise that quite simply, Awareness just IS and Awareness is the main game despite all the boxes I have ticked, tried to tick and not ticked. Even my pursuit of ticking boxes does not tick Awareness off!

Listen Clothing turned out to be quite a successful business, but after four years I was bored with it, and wanted to take the principles I had learned from the E Myth book and put them into action. I just didn't feel that Listen was the best company to do that with at the time.

Advanced Learning

One day I was in a fantastic bookstore called the Inspiration Factory browsing through their extensive selection of books when I bumped into a guy I knew called Richard Williams. "You've got to check out this book" he said excitedly, thrusting a copy into my hands. That book was the E Myth Revisited, by Michael Gerber possibly the greatest business book ever written. It's still sitting on various best seller lists after 40 years. From the moment I started reading the first pages I felt like the author was talking directly to me as a business owner.

The two main points that I took away from his book were:

1. Your business has to have a look and feel. It needs to be proprietary and have systems and procedures, and it needs to be replicable.

2. Great business owners don't necessarily do the work of the business, but instead they know how to run a business that does that work.

The Entrepreneurial Myth as Gerber described it was 'just because you know how to do the work of a particular business, doesn't mean that you also know how to run a business that does that work'. For example, the carpenter who sacks his boss to set up his own business assumes that he can run a carpentry business just because he knows how to be a carpenter.

Having read the *E Myth*, I was keen to put Gerber's ideas into practise. That's when I met Archie, a silicon clad plumber with lots of personality and a cheeky but very likeable disposition. Archie had come up with the business idea called *The Tap Doctor* and was running from the deep south to the most northern point of the Greater Perth area, servicing taps and doing plumbing work. He had four little black Honda Civics with taps on the roof – each loaded with tools - and was literally blowing their little engines up every other week through the sheer number of kilometres his vehicles were doing. Needless to say, he had no systems to optimise efficiency, nor did he have a way of keeping track of inventory or profitability.

I knew in my mind what this business needed to do! Having now read *The E-Myth* I was seeking a specific kind of business to apply all that advanced business learning to, and this was it. Of course, nothing happened in a straight line, but we were able to create a business which started selling franchises relating to demographic areas around Perth. This was soon expanded to include South Australia and then the rest of Australia. *The Tap Doctor* is still thriving today after nearly 30 years with the same Intellectual Property (IP) and the same look and feel, and I am always proud as I see the vans moving around the streets.

After five years building up the national franchise that *The Tap Doctor* had evolved into, I was still restless. I wanted more leverage and more speed, and I found this within public companies. After stockbroking I listed Insurance *My Way* during the dot com boom of the 1990s, which was a truly crazy time when companies' valuations would rise simply based on the announcement that were launching a website. The writing was on the wall that this boom was going to end badly but like so many stock market booms it lasted longer than most thought.

Insurance My Way, had raised $4m in its Initial Public Offering

(IPO) and it had not taken us long with above the line marketing, rent in the centre of the city and a large wages bill to work our way through those funds. Our saving grace as a company was that there was strong interest from a specialist private equity firm *before* the dot com crash and they had been doing due diligence on us for some four months. I remember the pivotal moment when everything came to a head, and we were given the opportunity to carry on as a business. We were sitting in our board room having an emergency meeting to decide if we needed to go into voluntary administration. Our chairman who was the CEO of one of Australia's major health funds at the time said: "let's just call them and ask".

He was referring to the private equity firm we had engaged with but who since the dot.com crash was giving us mixed messages. We needed an answer. Phil rang and gave it to them straight: "Are you going to invest in our company? Because if not we will be announcing voluntary administration."

The response came back within 24 hours in the affirmative. We were elated but still cautious. When the money hit our account several days later, we had the lifeline we needed to carry on. The stress of this situation was immense not only for the effect it had on me but also the many staff we employed. Conversely the relief was also immense for the private equity firm committing to the deal. That box of financial support that we had been working on for many months remained uncertain and with that 'thought' and its consequences came a stress. When the money landed in our bank account at that point the box was ticked, and all was 'well in the world'.

That business eventually pivoted into the energy sector and continues to be listed on the Australian Stock Exchange (ASX) some 20 plus years later.

Knowing Truth

*Even the most enlightened feel
resistance and suffering but they get back
on track and centred quicker than most.*

What is this thing we label procrastination – why am I putting off doing things like writing? I want to write my book, tell my story, teach my lessons but will anyone listen? Even me?

There is resistance, I recognise that. You could call it fear, putting off what should or must be done. We can break through, or we can see. I am a big fan of seeing what is before me.

I asked one of my teachers recently 'is there anything extra I can do to help me on my journey?' He answered: "Just watch yourself, watch everything you do. If you're driving watch that, if you're writing, watch yourself do that, if cycling, then focus on doing that and if procrastinating, then do that".

"What does this do?" I asked him.

"Well for one it begs the question who is observing, and who or what is procrastinating? To many this may sound like semantics, but it is far from that. The ability to observe is one of the extraordinary abilities and advantage that we have over other species."

Being the observer of your own life

I decided to focus on observing and inquiring. I started by asking myself: "what is this I am *feeling*, what is this I am *doing*?" Then I asked: "*who* is doing this, is this *true*, what's my *story*?"

You the reader might wonder why this is important. Well, it's because at the end of the asking is Truth! And as we know the Truth will set you free but first it will make you very angry!

The quote: "*The Truth will set you free*" is purported to have been written in the Bible by John the Baptist reporting on a message from Jesus Christ (John 8:32) when he addressed a gathering of Jews who believed he was the Messiah. An addendum to this has been developed by an unknown scribe who said that: "*The Truth will set you free, but first it will make you miserable!*"

The meaning behind this is simply the belief that Truth is something to avoid because it makes us miserable. The belief that truth will hurt us, hinder us, or make our lives unpleasant in some way.

Well, I say, first the truth will make you angry! Because Truth is not what we think it is.

The Truth is our ability to see,

and to see is to be free.

But what does this mean?

What we do and what we generally believe ourselves to be (the boxes we define ourselves by if you like) are autonomous to Self. It is the Self that observes these boxes for what they are, that they are relative truths. Discovering the Truth is discovering you are perfect but not in the way that you would think. Thinking actually has nothing to do with it!

The Truth is perfect, and yet the person you are is probably (if you're anything like me) very imperfect!

There is a podcast I recently stumbled across called Imperfects! Interestingly it is hosted by some very successful sports people, but they highlight that despite all appearances everyone has their struggles. And I mean everyone.

Our struggles are what point us towards the Truth.

Think of it this way, if there were no struggles why would we care about something, seemingly so esoteric? There is nothing esoteric about the Truth, despite the fact that we cannot touch it, feel it or see it, it is paradoxically the only thing that is not esoteric.

Our relative stories are linear – the Truth is not Linear – how could/can it be? Truth is everywhere. The Truth IS, it is not linear and cannot be described by the limited palate that is the mind. It is like using brushes to describe what paint is, without knowing that paint even existed in the first place. My point here is that the paint comes before the brush in the same way that Truth/Existence/Life comes before the thoughts, conditioning and stories we create.

So What?

In life we might go down many rabbit holes. We *have* experiences to help us make sense of everything as best we can. For every so-called negative connotation there likely to be a positive quality.

Each of these experiences leads me to understand that there is a connection between all the different sides of the same coins that have led me to question my experiences, understanding and life in general.

- Gullibility/Intuition
- Sugar hits/Inquisitiveness /A quest to learn.

- Avoiding Pain/Looking for answers
- Exhaustion/Hopelessness/Surrender
- Overly sensitive/Compassionate/Want to do the right thing.
- Lack of focus/Zest for all the things that are going on.

My journey, my expression is unique to me just as yours is unique to you. NO ONE can tell you that their journey is better than yours, more worthy that yours, more noble.

My point here is simply this. When you think you KNOW everything by its definition, you can find yourself believing that everyone else is less than you are in terms of their knowledge and understanding of it. You may feel that that you know best, and you finally have the keys to the universe. This is often evident in so called spiritual people, who have assumed the identity rather than the reality of what it truly means to be spiritual (this never ends by the way). There is no a specific place at which the genuinely spiritual person arrives and says I'm spiritual (another great paradox!!) Any identity assumed can be a great friend and in equal measure a great trap.

My kids sometimes say when I'm there I'll know. My wife and I ask, what do you mean by that, and they reply, 'you just know'. There is profound wisdom in this. It's true that when you know you know. It comes from a combination of faith, grit and, the best way to describe it, is that it's an inner Awareness of knowing that the underlying organising Truth that begets all things is pristinely whole, perfect and completely undefinable.

My job is to help people know they know, to remember and give them permission to remember!

Story On, Story Off!

Crank, Shlep, Crank

In my life I have been Amped then Still, Still then Amped and at times, neither Amped nor Still. The truth is we are always Still we just don't realise it or remember it.

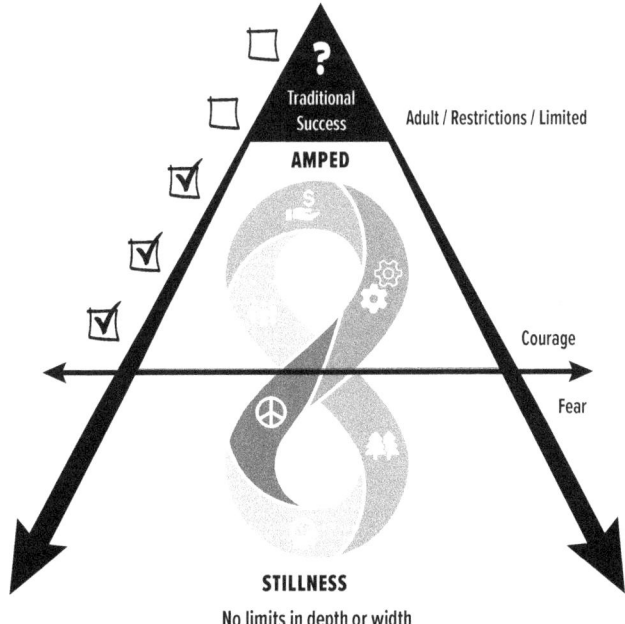

Our nervous system has been reconditioned and rewired to identify with everything but our inherent Stillness. Marketers, salespeople, our employers, our customers etc, all have a vested interest in keeping us Amped and moving, because they're all moving so fast, they want us to move and *that's how they perceive value in us.*

Our spiritual teachers want us to stop and reflect on what begets or comes before all this movement. This feels like relief for a while but if we stop moving for too long, the part of life that moves comes after us with stern reminders to pay the mortgage, put the kids through school or put new tires on the SUV.

The point is that we must not miss the *purpose* of our life which above all is to realise our True Nature. Most of us are just too busy staying Amped and living our lives to think about this but we must do this. Unfortunately, the very action of pausing to think has a tendency to throw our ignorant life or 'being asleep at the wheel' level of consciousness into chaos but still we *must* go there. Why? Because we need to experience that which *is* over that which is *not*. Again, it's a paradox, that which IS can't be seen, whereas that which IS NOT can be seen. That which *IS NOT* arises from that which IS, which again cannot be defined only KNOWN, EXPERIENCED, FELT.

The great saint Ramana Maharishi experienced the TRUTH as only that which is Permanent. His guidance practice is for his students to inquire into knowing: who are you? It is easier to say what is not permanent (as is done in a lot of tradition known as Neti Neti or not this, not that).

- Our Thoughts are not permanent.
- Our stories are not permanent.
- Our physical possessions are not permanent.
- Our physical body is not permanent.

So, what is permanent? That is the question, the journey and the destination!

I was talking to an old friend the other day and we were discussing how far his 15-year-old daughter has come from depression and self-doubt to a more confident young woman. Our discussion was precipitated by an article I saw in our major paper which highlighted an award-winning piece of art she had submitted. The art depicted tortured bodies and faces and was her interpretation of her struggle on her journey. From this torture she has emerged as an integrated and wise young artist. She still has to face her demons from time to time, as we all do, but she broke through some very uncomfortable and you could say 'dangerous' times. I was discussing with her dad just how proud he must be and it dawned on me that no real character is created without struggle! Her incredible character was born out of this dangerous scenario. Without struggle there is *no depth of character.*

My wife and I like to occasionally watch the sitcom Billions. One of the Billionaire characters in the series, Michael Prince, is approached by his two daughters, both in their 20s, in his fancy office. They talk to their dad and tell him how everyone from their university cohort is getting ahead and explain how they are at a serious disadvantage to the rest of their cohort because there is no struggle in their life. They say that because of him there are no consequences if they fail to make their own way and any door is open to them because of their standing and contacts in the community.

Imagine if your life was devoid of struggle. If everything was easy all the time, who would you be? What stories would you have in your boxes? How would you learn to handle adversity when you finally do need to face a major challenge in your life? Going back to what I said in chapter four around needing certainty; it comes down to growth, truth and what you are here to learn, do, be, have. How does your awareness and self-understanding guide you?

What tolerance do we have for struggle, and do we REALLY need it?

I believe we do. It's the resistance we need when building any muscle. For some people, it's the carbon that becomes a diamond. But in our modern world it is the stress which seems low grade and constant that also has the capacity to grind us down to dust.

Constant stress, lack of sleep, a poor diet, relationship pressures, financial concerns can all lead to negative issues of obesity, diabetes, cancer, mental health breakdowns, and round and round we go. The conveyor belt of life can appear very unfair and breaks people every day. One of the starkest examples is in the United States where (at the time of writing this) there have been five public massacres in as many weeks!

Can we just forgive and move on?

All of this is surely asking humanity to wake up! But what does this mean and how will it make any difference? My observation is that we kid ourselves that we change any issue in society by taking an action which our mind deems to be the right one. Take Covid for example – the rush to lock people down, vaccinating them whilst killing their businesses has caused so much collateral damage in terms of effects on mental health, finances and so much more. We couldn't wait to take action rather than stepping back and getting an understanding of what was really going on. Further to that we have been driven by the financial interests of major corporations and by some very wealthy individuals.

My job is to help people know they know, to remember and give them permission to remember!

Permission Givers

Allow even that!

What does it mean to be a Permission Giver?

In previous drafts of writing this book I always seemed to arrive at the same conclusion: the ultimate service is to be someone who through their actions gives others *permission* to live their best lives. I have often been blessed to have had enough awareness to recognise that if I am jealous of someone else's situation, I should take action to pursue that same thing and see if my envy was warranted. At the end of that I was not surprised to learn that most of the things I pursued in the name of jealously turned out to be relatively empty. But sitting with that emptiness again and again led to the recognition that the *relative* truth of the something can only make one *relatively* happy or fulfilled. I won't say I always get that right, but it's something I ponder and do my best to live with whenever I am aware of a notion of envy arising from a situation.

There are many different forms of permission giving. Someone who shows you how you can make a lot of money trading shares or doing a particular corporate deal or the health coach or doctor who shows you how to look after your health is effectively giving you permission to pursue that which you want to learn or investigate further. And then there's the permission giver of the spiritual kind.

Those great teachers who understand Truth and spend their lives in the service of others to help them realise their own Awareness.

I know a number of teachers who fall into this category. They may inspire you to wish you could be like them and then on closer examination you find that they are completely selfless! I don't know about you, but I'm not there yet. I still love my surfing, cycling, family time, coffees etc.

That's not to say you can't have these indulgences in life, those things that give you joy while you're also pursuing a deeper understanding of life and its meaning, but it can't be stressed enough that these incredibly selfless individuals only live for one thing: to serve in the name of a higher Truth that others have not yet realised. I'm talking about certain people. Spiritual beings walking among us who seem to be blessed with an even greater level of enlightenment and who wish only to share that.

How is any of this relevant? The answer is to be aware to what level and in what areas you are a Permission Giver. There are many parents, business leaders and health professionals who are incredible permission givers, including yourself. You just might not be seeing yourself that way.

This is a simple awareness that is carried throughout your day changing both the perception of yourself and those around you. There is a book series called the Go Givers[4] that focuses on the reverse philosophies of the Go Getters[5], that points to a similar theme and raises a point about the concept of opposite land. Rather than Go Get, Go Give – don't get permission, give permission!!

But how?

It keeps coming back to Self.

The Self has no boundaries, no fear, no boxes, no barriers. In

---

4 The Go Giver, by Bob Burg, John David Mann Penguin, 2010
5 Go Getters, by Peter K Byrne, 2022

fact, it has nothing of anything and yet it is the everything in every something.

What is this esoteric speak?

Well, it's esoteric until it's not.

It is only esoteric until it is a lived experience, whether glimpsed or experienced as a permanent knowing or reality like the great spiritual teachers both in the past and living.

Feel into your heart – what does it mean to be a Permission Giver? To me this is the ultimate act of service, to your spouse, your kids, your friends, your community and even those you have never met. As I sit here in the Typica Café, Perth and reflect on this Truth, it moves me to tears. When all is said and done, we are One in the Infinite Sun for Ever and Ever and Ever despite the fact that we appear separate. Everyone is acting separate, and it appears to be everyone for themselves - opposite land again!

As I look out the window of the café to my left, I see a man sitting in a wheelchair surrounded by what looks like his wife to his right and sitting opposite maybe his son and his sister (just guessing).

The gentleman in the wheelchair (his head slumped to one side and dribbling from his mouth) is being fed by his wife in a loving and patient way, she is not self-conscious or ashamed, she is serving! I looked across again just now and she is helping him drink from a straw with great patience and love. To me this is extraordinary permission giving. So simple, so profound.

Permission Giving is all around us. It is up to us to stay attuned to it, watch for the Permission Giver and learn from their example, so you may then follow suit with your unique expression.

Once this gentleman might have had a job. Someone might have called him boss, dad, friend, engineer etc. Has the state of his body now diminished who he really is? Is he any less?

This is a deep contemplation to which there is perhaps not a definitive answer. It is the questions we cannot answer that are the most deeply rooted in Truth. Like the question *Who are you?* Perhaps the deepest and most contemplative question of all.

Café Magic

A couple just came into the café holding hands - Permission Givers to each other.

Two hard looking men, each covered in tattoos embrace and hug with genuine warmth when one meets the other in this same café - Permission Givers. This is a concept that shatters stereotypes and informs us where we lack Awareness of our courage or otherwise.

More magic in the café as I observe a young man walking toward the entrance of the café on crutches, another slightly older gentleman with a nice soft energy sitting outside near the entrance gets up as the younger man approaches. Maybe they know each other – it's hard to be sure - but he is simply getting up to open the door for a man who might struggle to open the door himself today.

The greatest influencers are Permission Givers. They certainly have been in my life, and they can come in all forms. You could get your permission by someone denying you something. We have a number of life lessons from the Dalai Lama on a mural hanging in our home. One of the lessons says: *Be grateful for the opportunities you miss out on or the things you are denied.* Perhaps this is giving you permission to move in another direction, because in fact denial and tragedy seem to drive us in our most purposeful directions which often, we only can see and appreciate with the benefit of hindsight.

The Line of Courage

Get there by being here!

In the Amped Stillness Model our objective is to lead a life full of achievements and fulfillment. The line that sits between the two triangles in the model I originally labelled the Line of Fear. This is because our fear of letting go of all that is known. But as the model evolved, I changed this line to The Line of Courage and of course Courage does not exist without fear, so it really is just the other side of the same coin.

The Line of Courage is really about building the muscle of awareness, activating the part of the brain that is more tuned into Self and less associated with fight or flight.

The Line of Courage is Really the Courage to See.

Integrity is the ability to admit everything to yourself. By everything I mean your motives for what you do, how you feel. You don't have to reveal your motives to everyone around you, just to yourself. For example, if you're doing a job, you hate doing but you need the money, admit to yourself you're doing the job for the money. If you see someone in a fancy car and you wished you had the same car, admit to yourself you feel jealous or angry or impatient. Go deeper with that and explore it. As I said in the last chapter, it might well be that you come to see the relative truth of something is only relative to your happiness in what it is you desire *in that moment.*

We had some plants delivered to our house the other day and the delivery person said in an extremely blunt way that there was no way he was bringing his truck down our fairly narrow lane. I explained to him that other big trucks had come down the lane with no incident in recent days, to which he replied:

"The sun produces a billion kw of energy and light every day which is also a fact but I'm not bringing my fucking truck down the lane."

Just after I very briefly visualised a 'very inappropriate' way to respond I felt a complete calm come over me. I was able to observe that this conversation was going nowhere and that I had to find another solution as to how to get the plants into our back yard. It didn't feel like thinking, but more like an instant awareness that there was no need to *be right* but just to deal with the current reality. I was also aware of my need to see my reaction to it. I don't know about you, but I am faced with these types of challenges every day and it provides great Awareness training.

Through being *Aware* and using my discretion to not react as I intrinsically knew that to do so would be futile at best and dangerous at worst. When you are Aware, you just know!

24 Hours of Insights

In the last 24 hours a number of things happened where I found myself able to register the awareness of being the observer in the moment.

- The coffee house I visited provided additional awareness training by taking a long-time delivering coffee and offering poor service. I exercised patience and focused on my awareness of all that was going on for them, everyone around me, and myself in those minutes and was grateful for the pause in my day instead of grumbling about the delay.
- I encountered a driver not going immediately into the flow of traffic after I waved them in - which would normally have adjusted my inner frustration over his resistance to my kindness.
- My son called me constantly to talk about his travel plans whilst I was trying to watch my beloved Giro D'talia cycle race, and I found myself able to easily not berate him for his terrible timing but instead to appreciate his wanting my time and my advice.
- My wife wanted to have conversations about house building plans late at night when I was tired, and I was able to put her needs ahead of my own to have that conversation. I saw feeling more focused on her needs as a great way to end my day, not as an intrusion into my tiredness.

You get the picture, there are so many times a day where we stand at the Line of Courage and choose whether we are going to react in awareness from a point of Courage or drift back into an unconscious, conditioned state.

The Line of Courage has two edges – the material world (that world we typically call real) and the unseen world, that from which everything is created and ultimately goes back to.

The awareness of the unseen world is REAL. It is our greatest ally when we apply the Line of Courage to our principal of Awareness. Sitting in your reality, developing the ability to be conscious in every moment, watching what you're doing and why, and being brutally honest with yourself is powerful. Being honest about your motives, stopping the pretence that you are virtuous and good in every way is ultimately a way we can move past the trickery of our minds which will do anything to keep us safe and right.

How can our story always be the right story?

As we have seen, at best our stories are a relative truth.

Beyond the Boxes

The biggest obstacle to a great life is a good life.

When we confine our lives within the small compartments of our Big Box, our true identity becomes clouded. Instead of perceiving and experiencing the world as it truly is, we see it through the lens of our own context. It's like viewing the world through customized glasses that tinge everything we see. This perspective becomes ingrained in us, much like when we're intoxicated, which alters our perception and leads us to behave in ways we otherwise wouldn't.

However, if we can recognize and embrace our true selves as the container that holds *all* our stories, there is no need to attach ourselves to specific identities or labels. Our individual boxes still hold significance as they encapsulate our so-called achievements, failures, and the narratives we have constructed around them. However, there is never lasting fulfillment in accomplishments. Achievements within each of our smaller boxes are fleeting. In contrast, our Big Box presents an opportunity for profound understanding, where everything is inherently perfect.

Let us now delve into the immaculate and inseparable nature of the Box that encompasses everything, untouched by external influences.

My First Sweat Lodge

I attended my first Sweat Lodge about 27 years ago as part of a special Men's Retreat follow up course from a *Future Warrior* course. There was a bit of an introduction where Brendan the facilitator and founder of both courses explained how he was drawn to native American culture and went in search of his first Sweat Lodge in Colorado, in the US. He went to a local café in the town of Durango and found a group of native Americans and explained to the group respectfully that if possible, he would like to attend Sweat Lodge of Inipi ceremony to which one of the men said 'run up and down the street a few times, that will get you sweating!' Brendan laughed, demonstrating the first test of character they had placed before him. Not long after that, the same gentleman who had made the comment, noticed the person who provided the wood walking into the café – to him this was a sign the planets had aligned to make this Lodge happen. He looked Brendan in the eye and said with intensity: "Tomorrow at 1PM, Sweat Lodge in your honour".

Some 15 years later and after attending many Lodges myself I started offering a form of the Sweat Lodge ceremony in the Southwest of Western Australia. I have now been 'pouring' Sweat Lodges from the same location for over 10 years, which many people tell me is the most profound experience of their life.

The experience is one of sacrifice. It gets very hot, it's dark and you're sitting on a muddy earth floor, which for most Westerners is very unfamiliar, and that's what makes it both mysterious and special. I have found there is great freedom in leaping into the unknown and shaking off the day to day we live over and over again.

There are many forms of the Sweat Lodge, but the type I am most familiar with is based on the Lakota Sioux way which involves a dome shaped tent (the Lodge) which is pitch black inside and has a pit in the middle. Participants sit inside the tent around the perimeter.

Outside the Lodge, 19 rocks sit in a blazing fire; these are arranged and blessed in a sacred way. Over four rounds the rocks are brought inside the darkened space, each round represents a different part of each person participating in the ceremony.

1. First the rocks that have been in the fire are recognised and blessed,

2. Prayers for oneself and circumstances and own cleansing,

3. Prayers for healing,

4. Prayers of thanks and gratitude are given.

Sweat Lodges are one of those things you will never forget and can help all connect more deeply and experience that we are one in the infinite sun for ever and ever.

Vision Quest

It seems many of the native American ceremonies I have drawn to have similar themes of:

- Give something of yourself,
- Suffer a little or a lot (as the case may be),
- Confront your deepest fears and demons and,
- Break through, shattering your conditioning about what you thought was possible with the help of your higher Self,
- Discovering you are this Self and ultimately realising that this Nothingness/Everythingness is who you are and can be relied on.

The Lakota name for the Vision Quest is Hanbleceya and entails spending four days in the open wilderness with no shelter or food, praying for a Vision.

I have done one Vision Quest and during my four days in the elements I experienced many profound things including 'experiencing being a tree', having a small joey run straight into me (this actually happened) and many other things. The most noticeable thing was just how much chatter and suffering I created through my Monkey Mind, which only started to die down after about the third day.

Sundance

Sundance is another Native American Ceremony and whilst I have not done one myself, I have supported a friend who has. Suffice to say that Sundance is one of the most sacred of ceremonies which involves dancing without food or water for four days in the baking sun whilst being connected to a tree for at least some of that time. Many of these ceremonies boggle the mind; they don't seem to make sense until you experience them or see them in action, at which point they reveal something so simple and profound and equally perplexing to the mind. These ceremonies seem to trick the mind into giving up its racket.

The ultimate outcomes for anyone participating in these ceremonies is also to identify that *nothingness* and *everythingness* is who you are, and what you can rely on. The concept of Stillness and Being is enhanced by the process of learning to experience the pureness of your naked and vulnerable self. By naked, I mean open and exposed with fears being met, spiritual guidance being leaned into and being able to step outside of your own body to view who you really are in deep and profound ways.

If you are to obtain that which you seek at your soul levels, then you must understand that you can only get there, by being here. That the secret to getting everything you really want lies in being who you really are.

The Amped Stillness Model is focused on the interconnectedness of what lies above the line – the boxes you tick as you go through life seeking to be who you are - to circling back to seeking your enlightenment by going below the line and facing your fears, and understanding there really is no formula, no finish line and nowhere to go. Below the line there is nothing to understand because all is simply not understandable. You can only *realise* it.

Learning to live your life both above and below the line, means you move between your story being on, and your story being off or as stated above, simply being integrated into it.

When You Need the Lessons – They Will Come to You

My friend Nick* seemed to have it all. He had attended one of the finest universities in the US after which he went on to join an investment bank where he worked hard, but with that came the rewards of a lifestyle from the sort of income that that make most people's eyes water. By the time he turned 50, he was married with three children, owned a holiday home in Connecticut, and many other fine toys and testaments to his success. But the pressures of business, children and marriage for over 26 years were starting to get to him. One of the bigger issues he was coping with over a number of years was that his eldest child was challenged with serious mental health issues and despite being incredibly smart and herself being granted access to the finest university in the country, she had been sectioned a number of times in a mental institution. She was self-harming in horrible ways, a symptom of the self-hatred she had for herself.

Nick had started seeing another woman; something he described as a symptom of his failing relationship with his wife rather than as a straight-out affair. It started out as a very platonic but close friendship however his wife was very unhappy about this, and they eventually decided for the sake of everyone he must leave the family home.

His wife was distraught, as she hadn't foreseen the level of unhappiness Nick was experiencing within their relationship, and certainly didn't understand it. From the kids' perspective, Dad was being irrational, unfair and selfish, they were confused and very angry at his actions. Nothing he could say would console them or help them understand. As far as they were concerned there was something wrong with him, he needed to come to his senses and fast.

Nick was numb and confused himself, had he tried hard enough? Was he a bad person? In the months leading up to his starting to see this other woman he had wanted something in his life to "break". Was it a form of unconscious self-sabotage or a more deliberate move to grow and help get his life back on some sort of track perhaps with higher meaning. The friend with whom he'd kept relatively quiet about until it all blew up, did become his new partner after the breakdown of his marriage, and she had also recently split from a relationship which was dysfunctional and violent at times. They found consolation in each other, but Nick had things in his old world that he could not run away from.

Nick had ticked all the outer boxes in his life. And yet despite those many levels of success he still couldn't find what he was looking for. He felt dead inside. The destruction of his world as he had known it was overwhelming and shocking. Navigating a new world he was unfamiliar with left him reeling with self-doubt, finding it hard to know what would come next. Waves of increasing dysfunction rolled his world, with ever increasing instability. There was also of course the challenge Nick's wife faced being left behind without him – her former husband, best friend and confidante - to confide in or to lean on emotionally, while their children continued to rail against the changes thrust upon them through this breakup. The emotional pain and suffering seemed unbearable for everyone.

This is a common mess for many people in relationships. How do we break something that's not working in a responsible and empathetic way? Is it even possible? It is clear it's not an exact science and this wrecking (if you like) of our old world can be a blessing but only when we learn the ground rules for the next phases of our life.

For Nick and his family, their new situation presented opportunities but there was also emotional dangers and a lot of stuff to sort out. Life had never been this messy for Nick and the old systems that he had used to get so much external success and recognition simply did not work in his new reality.

When faced with uncertainty, it is human nature to fight against change and disruption. It takes time to allow what *is*, and what *is* not. But when we do surrender and allow discomfort, then we begin to let life, the moment, and the forces outside of our actual control start to do the heavy lifting for us. Surrender is something that does not come naturally, regardless of how hard we rail against change, we eventually realise that change *is* what we need in order to grow.

No matter how certain any of our lives may ever be on a day-to-day basis, there is never any guarantee that unpredictable, messy and disruptive torrents will not come along at any time and leave us reeling in the mess left behind. But recognizing that it really is a natural force that is there for the purpose of allowing us to learn to lean in and let go helps. It's like swimming against a rip tide, vs swimming with it but knowing we can still make it safely to shore if we relax and stop exhausting ourselves against the current.

The Final Word
Life Lived in Amped Stillness

*The shift from Movement to Stillness
can be challenging because we experience
the dynamic nature of the mind not
the Truth / Stillness*

If we get lucky in life, our misfortunes and failures will drive us to take a look inside ourselves to reveal the Awareness or Stillness that is intelligent and pristine. It never judges, places condition or has a view; this is simply who we ultimately are and is what every truly wise person points to as the purpose of life. That is to discover our True Nature. Only you can determine if this is something that carries any importance for you.

You may or may not be ready to discover your True Nature and what does that even mean right? Well, one of the key messages of this book is that it's your job and no one else's to find out. Why? Because Life will seem purposeful as a result.

But your life already has purpose. I am here to raise my kids, grow my business, be a good partner, friend, boss, leader... I hear you say this and that is true but all those purposes you currently have are transient. The kids will grow up, you'll retire from that job, that relationship reach new stages, you'll no longer be able to do that physical activity at some point in time.

You may argue: "So what! I'll find something else!"

As it happens disillusion is our best friend, this about the word: Dis – illusion, don't we all want to be Dis – Illusioned? Maybe not because that would mean having to face many of the things we have been covering up. We use illusion to cover the uncomfortable things we see in ourselves and others.

If we are to be truly at peace and joyful, we must become *dis*-illusioned and fully aware of ourselves with the perspective of Stillness and Truth.

Some time ago I came up with the phrase Personal Diminishment, which in many ways is a far more useful description than personal development. Personal development is all about making the ego-self more robust and less breakable, which has its place. We must develop self to achieve above the line, but we must also diminish the importance we place on the seen part of our life and place even more importance on the invisible intelligence that begets all things i.e. the Stillness.

Personal development is like moving the deck chairs on the Titanic and expecting everything to be ok.

The issue is that when we use our above the line strategies and tactics to try to 'find' the fundamental Still Intelligence we are on a hiding to nothing because by definition our mind *separates* and defines everything. 'Still Wisdom' is everywhere and undividable and because it is the mind's job to define, it cannot experience the undefinable/undividable.

It is like asking the prison warden to free the prisoner, but it's not the prison warden's job to release the prisoner, it's their job to keep the prisoner locked up. In that same way it's the mind's job to keep the Universal Intelligent Stillness from being experienced.

So, where to from here?

Well, that very much depends on you, regardless of anything and anyone, your history, your upbringing, your background; you are in charge, it just might not feel like it. There is an opportunity to go on a journey of simultaneous growth and diminishment. However, this is the paradox of a fulfilling life; we are doing both at the same time which is what the Amped Stillness model represents. Of course, the Amped Stillness model is not *The Truth* but is rather a bridge to try to save you time. Whether it ultimately does this will depend on many variables – always personal to each of us. It seems the more we understand, the more we feel like we really don't know.

The Bridge

We need our minds and thinking to conceive of a better Life within a larger context and Truth. This intellectual exercise of looking for something bigger that gives our life meaning is not experienced and ultimately 'experiencing' Stillness as the Truth, or more accurately our True Nature, is what matters. Why does it matter? Because Stillness is not movement and this matters because thoughts are in constant movement. And if we're always moving, in our minds how do we ever have a point of reference to make good decisions and take right action? When we have a Stillness reference point Life becomes so much easier to navigate because it is only from a vantage point of Stillness that we can recognise what needs to be done in any moment.

When we are making important decisions in our life we get Still (without the influence of our constant thoughts) and our decisions arise as an intuition to take the right action and then we act with full conviction. We go for it knowing that our decision was made with the support of a larger force – 'Stillness'.

When I watched Game of Thrones (GOT) several years ago it used to amaze me how some of the characters would face great adversity, carry on and get up and face challenge after challenge. We can learn how to watch the challenges of our life like movies - somewhat remotely knowing that whatever we face on our journey it's likely to change at some point. If we don't have a Stillness reference point in this turbulent dynamic world, we're going to suffer with every little adverse thing that happens. To transcend that Suffering we must have that Stillness point from which we view all else, like a movie. Just like watching GOT.

We go out to go in, and go in to go out; both sides of the coin serve one another in a beautifully perfect way. We need to apply more energy to going IN because everything in our day-to-day activities tend to drag us OUT, (above the line) to tick boxes, get things done and show the world how successful we are by that which we can touch feel and define.

The Core Message of this Book

What is the most effective way to live our life? On my journey I've observed that there are people who want to live a 'spiritual' life and don't want to engage with the world. These are often those of us who have watched the Secret one too many times and thinks they can manifest their dreams without actually doing anything. Then there are those that are just doing, doing, doing the whole time, petrified that if they stop, they will perish in unimportance.

There is a fundamental belief by most of us that it is our perpetual movement which gives us meaning and purpose.

In this book we look at both approaches and ultimately realise that there is no separation in anything. However, in order to really understand this, it can be helpful to separate that which is NOW

- indescribable and mysterious - from that which we can define, is concrete, and which we can create stories around. The book captures this concept in the Amped Stillness Model, which points to the profound, beauty of the path we walk.

Ultimately this book points to the Truth that there is no right or wrong, just the path we are walking. We have become separated from our True Nature, it is our job to reconnect and rediscover our inherent nature, which is Oneness.

No matter what we've done, what boxes we have ticked, no matter what we've achieved or not achieved or what people have to say about us, our True Nature is independent and lies dormant waiting for us to realise we are that.

As much as we dissect and analyse our life, we are ONE.

The purpose of this book is to help you, the reader, build a bridge from Stillness to Movement and then back again. The outside world gives us real time feedback on the consequences of our decisions, and our Stillness facilitates by giving us a seat, a point of reference which is intelligent, calm and blissful -- the antithesis of everything that moves.

Acknowledgements

There are a number of people I need to acknowledge in the writing of this book. First and foremost, my wife Antonia who always supports me when I have lofty ideas and is the best wife and mother to our children anyone could wish for. I want to thank my threes kids for being who they are and making our life ever interesting through the ups and downs, it's a privilege for us to help you on your journeys as you do us.

To my parents Ron and Sandra who are always there for the whole family and provide a template from which to build a remarkable life full of achievement, empathy and Love. Your good nature and persistence and enthusiasm to always create something new and better is an inspiration to so many.

To my business mentor Craig Burton who toughened me and softened me all at once, thanks for showing me the complexities of business and work and how the material world works.

To my Guru, ShantiMayi who is uncompromising in living and teaching Truth. Thank you for always supporting me and loving me unconditionally, you are Permission Giver of the highest order. Your unconditional Love is unwavering, and heart felt.

To Stuart Mooney who introduced to Sri Vidya meditation and has been a guide for many years. Thank you for your generosity and commitment to teaching and demonstrating the highest expression of Truth.

To Mukti my teacher and humble loveable brother who has taught me so much about Native American culture and life.

To Brendan Nichols who was a teacher in the early years of my journey, thanks for igniting my passion for the love of personal and spiritual growth.

To all my friends and work colleagues over the years that have been integral to an incredible journey so far, thanks for your love support and humor.

Lastly thank you to my book coach Dixie. Thanks for your patience, belief and constant coaxing and for being that iron fist in a velvet glove. We did it!

"Tim-isms"

"Until you lose something, you really don't know what its value was."

"The biggest obstacle to a great life is a good life."

"We've all heard the saying, what doesn't kill you makes you stronger. Acne made me realize that there has to be more to life than the physical."

"Are you ready to explore who you are when your stressful thoughts are un-tied?"

"The real secret to transformation is realizing you don't need the carrot and the stick to take action."

"Above the line is movement, below the line is Stillness, which is intelligent, blissful, and True."

"If you can't experience Stillness, you are always navigating life from a perspective that is moving and changing."

"Discovering Stillness may not be a straight line, which is why we need courage."

"Our mind tends to follow it, create stories around it, and draw natural conclusions based on the evidence we created from our previous observed experience."

About Tim Wise

Tim Wise is an Australian author, entrepreneur, and seeker of wisdom whose life journey and experiences have profoundly shaped his perspectives on success and fulfilment. Born into a family with a history of resilience and entrepreneurship, Tim's upbringing was marked by a blend of love, hard work, and the legacy of his immigrant grandparents who instilled in him a deep appreciation for the opportunities life offered.

Despite his successful business ventures, Tim's true calling has always been in exploring the depths of personal and spiritual development. From suffering severe acne as a teenager, which spurred his initial quest for deeper meanings in life, to his transformative experiences with spiritual masters in India, Tim's journey is a compelling testament to the power of self-discovery.

Over the years, Tim has dedicated himself to understanding the nuances of what it truly means to live a fulfilled life beyond societal expectations. His writings, including "Surviving Success," reflect his commitment to helping others navigate the complexities of personal identity, happiness, and inner peace. With his unique blend of entrepreneurial spirit and profound spiritual insights, Tim Wise continues to inspire readers to explore the profound journey of self-realization and to redefine their own measures of success.

Wanting to know more?

If you would like to find out more about Tim Wise, engage him to speak at your next event, or discuss mentoring or Sweat Lodge opportunities, please visit his website:

www.timwise.com   or   www.anskeya.com.au

www.ingramcontent.com/pod-product-compliance
Lightning Source LLC
Chambersburg PA
CBHW061739070526
44585CB00024B/2742